Eagle County Airport

S0-AVQ-047

Photo © Brent Bingham

History of Eagle County Airport:
How Love of Aviation Formed the Airport

Acknowledgements

The Eagle County Aviation Association sincerely acknowledges the efforts and dedication of many people who have contributed to this book.

This book would not have been written without the prompting of Jim Driver. Jim and Merritt Moselle dedicated decades of aviation knowledge and work compiling articles and information on the history of the Eagle County Regional Airport. Jim has written a reference book for the local Historical Society which served as a research foundation for this book. Jim served several years at the Flight Service Station at EGE, aiding pilots and passengers alike, before a dedicated control tower was added to the airfield. Jim's love of this airport and dedication to aviation make him one of the reasons why this airport is so great.

This book would not be possible without the determination and dedication of Jennifer (Jena) L. Taylor, "The Word Tailor". Jena took the initial research information and brought the historical events to life by interviewing numerous individuals, locating additional photos and articles, as well as verifying the book's factual information and data. Jena worked closely with John Oleson, Allan and Celeste Nottingham, Leonard Sinclair, Jim Driver, Mike Lederhause, Hugo and Jacki Benson, Casey Frehe, Steve Isom, Craig Colby, Major Joshua Day, Kent Meyers, Mike Zimpel, Dick Gustafson, Lee Weatherbee, Charlynn Williams, Chris Anderson, Jim Allen, and Paul Gordon to bring us this book.

Without Mike Lederhause reviving membership in the ECAA, and he and his wife Edith's constant efforts to keep the ECAA going, this book would not have come to fruition. Mike dedicated hours to the meticulous editing of this book. Without Mike's knowledge of aviation and experience at the airport, this book would not have come together as well as it did.

We dedicate this book to those people who have a love for aviation and a great deal of passion for the place we call the Eagle County Regional Airport.

The Eagle County Aviation Association

History of Eagle County Airport:
How Love of Aviation Formed the Airport

Jennifer L. Taylor and
Eagle County Aviation Association

This book was generously underwritten by
Eagle County Aviation Association, Vail Valley Jet Center, and Eagle County

Wings Publishing, Inc.

Publication Information

Copyright © 2007 by Eagle County Aviation Association.

All rights reserved

Library of Congress Cataloging-in-Publication Data:
Eagle County Aviation Association.
    History of Eagle County Airport: How Love of
    Aviation Formed the Airport
      p.   cm.
    ISBN 0-9771136-1-2. 978-0-9771136-1-3
  1. Eagle County Colorado Airport – Eagle County
    Regional Airport 2. Local History of Aviation

Printed in the United States of America

First printing: June 2007

Published by The Old Gypsum Printer, Inc.,
aka Wings Publishing, P.O. Box 270, Gypsum, CO 81637
www.oldgypsumprinter.com

Design and layout by Terri Lowery of "2 Rivers Design",
Moline IL

Photographs courtesy of Eagle County Historical Society, Eagle County Regional Airport, Vail Valley Jet Center, John Oleson, Mike Lederhause, and Allan Nottingham, if not noted specifically.

Authors	**Eagle County Aviation Association**
	Jennifer L. Taylor
Design/Layout	**Terri Lowery**
Editor	**Jennifer L. Taylor**
Researchers	**Jim Driver**
	Jennifer L. Taylor
Cover Photography	**Brent Bingham**

Jennifer L. Taylor is a freelance writer residing in Granby, CO. Contributors for this publication include Jim Driver, who performed initial research and provided editing comments; and Terri Lowery, whose unending patience during copy and layout changes and creative skills are greatly appreciated.

Table of Contents

Welcome

"The airport runway is the most important main street in any town."
—Norm Crabtree, Former Deputy Director, Division of Aviation

The rich history of the Eagle County Airport is due to the dreams of many, beginning with the pioneers of aviation in Eagle County to those who dream of improvements and advancements that lie ahead. Like most communities, the Eagle County Airport (EGE) links Eagle Valley to the rest of the world. This link has brought much growth and prosperity to our community.

Many have worked to tell the story of the evolution of our airport from its beginnings as a model airplane landing strip to the modern and sophisticated airport it is today. As the airport reaches its 60th anniversary, we decided it was time to tell the story of the history of the airport while people could still provide living history testimony.

We hope that you enjoy the journey through time as we present the story of how EGE came to be and may you enjoy your journey as you travel through our airport and community as much as we enjoy flying based out of EGE.

—Eagle County Aviation Association

Jule Oleson, right, with unidentified [mechanic],
circa 1921 in front of Jule's Waterman Type 3C100 airplane

A Humble Beginning

Using trick photography, Ed Belding and Eldon Wilson pose with model airplane, 1939

The history of the airport traces back to the early 1900s. County records indicate that in 1911, Louise Ellen Cooley purchased 650 acres of land from Hans Oleson. This land lies under the present runway complex at EGE.[1] Testimony and early records indicate that barnstormers like Fred Gray occasionally landed here and offered rides to the public for about $3/ride flying Army Surplus Curtiss Robins and JN4 Jenny planes in the late 1920s and 1930s. As early as 1931, there was much interest in the airport for the purpose of air mail and passenger traffic connecting Denver to Western Colorado.[2] Dr. O.W. Randall headed a committee that included A.B. Koonce, Tom Doran, and G.G. Rice, to explore establishing a landing strip or air field.[3]

In the early 1920s, brothers Victor Julius (Jule) Oleson and Albert (Al) Oleson owned the first airplanes in Western Colorado. They built a hangar on their family property that is now in the area near Jules Drive in Gypsum, and flew out of there using a dirt landing strip that is on the mesa west of the current airport.[4] The first airplane Jule owned was purchased from Walter M. Ainsley, of Glenwood Springs, CO, for $6,000, of which Jule paid cash.[5] The airplane is described in the bill of sale as being "new" and of "first-class condition" and could "operate with a full load of three persons, or a useful load of 715 pounds, from a field 6,500 feet above sea level, and climb with said load to a ceiling of 14,000 feet above sea level".[6] A 1921 *Eagle Valley Enterprise* article claims that "V.J. Oleson...announced plans to become

These two photos belonged to John Oleson's mother. Unfortunately, the photos were not documented.

the first Eagle County aviator to be based here".[7] Jule said that he "intended to use the plane for commercial purposes between valley towns, carrying passengers and demonstrating stunt flying.[8] When Albert's son Jack was born in 1925, the plane was "gone". As the family recalls, Al & Jule crashed the plane somewhere and just walked away from it.[9]

In the late 1930s, Eldon Wilson, Ed Belding, and Harold "Mick" Randall created a model airplane landing area and staked out a dirt landing strip 0.6 miles long x 300' wide,[10] (where High Altitude ARNG Training Site hangar is now located). Developments started moving along in 1933 when Harry A. Nottingham, early airport supporter, began his term as County Commissioner. In 1939, E.G. Barry, Federal District Airport Engineer, stated to Eldon Wilson "their search for an airport between Leadville and Grand Junction was over".[11] The site on Cooley Mesa was selected because of its absence of the typical hazards: wires, trees, or close proximity to high mountains.

In that same year, Eldon Wilson and County Commissioner Wayne T. Jones borrowed equipment again to create a "good road" built for under $20 to access the landing strip.[12] Around 1942, the

"Eldon Wilson was the visionary who pushed the airport along."
– Harold Koonce

CAA (Civil Aeronautics Administration, the precursor to FAA) acquired airport property then belonging to the Herin family.[13] The property was leveled and an emergency grass landing strip about 300' wide x 3000' long was created to ferry military airplanes across the country.[14] The United States participated in the Alaska-Siberia Lend-Lease program, part of which included ferrying airplanes from the lower 48 states to Alaska.[15] Once the aircraft arrived in Alaska, Russian pilots flew them across the Bering Strait to their homeland to combat Nazi Germany.[16] According to documentation, the only plane that needed to use it was one B-25 Bomber.[17] In 1945, the CAA designated the Castle Range north of Eagle as the spot for the radio beam range and construction of the beacon was started at an altitude of 9000 feet.[18]

On Dec. 4, 1945, Eagle County, through the work of the Eagle County Commissioners, purchased 111.23 acres of the original Cooley property from Charles Hemberger and George R. Spangler for $1,390 and began to maintain the airfield at an expense of approximately $300 per year.[19] The government purchased land from Mrs. Grace Oleson earlier.

With plans in place to build a modern airport, the FSS (Flight Service Station) was commissioned on January 1, 1946.[20] At the time, the airstrip was just gravel and grass. The Flight Service Station provided

Eldon Wilson

John Coffey, standing, and Jim Driver

weather advisories to aircraft flying over central Colorado as well as the arriving and departing aircraft at EGE. The FSS provided 24-hour service until it was closed in 1994 and its functions were transferred to the consolidated FSS near Denver, CO. A temporary control tower was then placed in operation at EGE. Grant Brallier was an early leader of the group of controllers and staff who were not only FSS employees but were long-time residents of Eagle Valley. Staff members George Chandler, Paul Lindstrom, Robbie Robinson, John Coffey, Jim Driver, and Stella Meyers were some of the many folks that operated the FSS facility. Pappy Haggert maintained the facilities at Red Hill, Corona Pass, and Castle Peak in addition to the airport.

Allan Nottingham remembers how comforting it was to call George Chandler, or whomever was working, to determine what the conditions were and if Castle Peak or Red Hill were socked in or not. A lot of the time this meant a phone call from Denver, Grand Junction, or Montrose. Allan remembers, "This was a long time before NWS (National Weather Service) could give any conditions at EGE. In my 40 years of flying in and out of EGE, I found [the FSS] services invaluable." Providing this service also

FSS 1984 (Courtesy Cheryl Krieger)

> Bob Deane used to say frequently: "You gotta watch it out there.
> There's rocks in them clouds."

developed some close friendships. Allan fondly recalls, "I remember George joking, 'Boy, you made a couple or three landings that time!'" George Chandler was at FSS from 1958-1975.

Allan Nottingham leased his first plane in 1962 and kept it parked at the airport in the summer of 1963. In 1964, he purchased his first airplane, a 1954 Cessna 180, an airplane he still owns and flies today. This Cessna has been based at EGE since 1964. Allan took his airplane to the East Slope for a few winters until 1968 and it has been at EGE full-time since then.[21]

Other early aviators at EGE include Bob Deane and Fred Collett. Bob Deane used to say frequently: "You gotta watch it out there. There's rocks in them clouds." Fred Collett flew out of EGE from about 1960-2003 and organized many air shows and events.

The big day finally came on September 14, 1947 when the airport was officially dedicated as Eagle County Airfield.[22]

Allan Nottingham with his plane, November 1989

In 1961, Eagle County applied to the FAA for transfer of lighting facilities of the airport to Eagle County.[23] County Commissioner Chairman Harry Nottingham proposed a runway 60' wide x 5300' long. Mr. Nottingham correctly predicted that "a better airport will be a boon to Eagle County...air travel is constantly increasing, and if we have modern landing facilities, we can attract many more hunters, fishermen, and even skiers into our area...".[24] The estimated cost to complete this was $15,000.[25] Harry Nottingham was County Commissioner for 28 years and was instrumental in the initial paved landing strip as well as other airport development between the years of 1932 and 1964.

Harry Nottingham

On January 1, 1962, A.E. Horning, Chief of FAA Aviation Facilities Division, noted in a letter to Walt Swanson, Eagle Valley Aviation member "that the County of Eagle is preparing to take over ownership and operation" of the landing field.[26] The gravel and dirt runway was replaced by a 50' wide x 5000' long asphalt runway. (Note: there was no taxiway at this time.)[27] This runway was called 8/26. The precursor to modern commercial flights first arrived at EGE in January 1966 when Rocky Mountain Airways of Denver opened an office for its Vail Airways.

Improvements were required in 1966 in order to meet the demands of the FAA to provide 24-hour weather and radio reporting as they were not equipped to perform arrivals and departures under adverse weather conditions. After research and analysis, an all-weather operation was determined possible and a non-directional beacon was bought from Frontier Airlines and installed. This established for the first time a direct air route between Denver and Eagle with instrument approach facilities and procedures for all weather arrivals and departures.[28]

Mountain Flying Services opened for business in July 1973.

In June 1966, Eagle County residents urged County Commissioners to update the airfield. Air traffic at the field had increased from an average of one flight/day to more than four flights/day in the previous two years and added that it would be "an economic benefit to the county".[29] Also in that same year, Rocky Mountain Airways announced two flights daily from Denver to Eagle.[30] In 1967, Vail Airways filed requests to extend services from Denver via EGE to Aspen.[31]

Additional improvements came when William F. Stevens built the first paved hangar in 1968. Dick Bailey and Trevor Bradway also followed suit shortly thereafter.[32] This was also

John Oleson

the year that serendipity intervened in John Oleson's life plan and his vision set the foundation for the future success of EGE. John approached Mr. Stevens with his plan of establishing an FBO after they saw a need for more services at the growing airport. John began by flying chartered planes as well as giving lessons. Mr. Stevens financed the efforts and the idea of Mountain Flying Services was born.[33] One of John Oleson's first students was Bill Nottingham.[34]

In 1969, Business at the airport was booming as Rocky Mountain Airways (formerly Vail Airways) began five daily flights to Eagle and ordered three Fairchild-Swearingen 225 jet-prop transports.[35] The plane seated 20 people, each with a window, plus 2 crew members and traveled at 300 mph+ with a travel time of 30 minutes from Denver to Eagle. This development allowed Vail to become a four-season resort with year-round flights available to its customers.[36]

In July of 1973 the County approved their lease and John Oleson, with his business partner William F. Stevens, officially opened the FBO in a double wide trailer, offering aviation fuel, rental cars and van service to the local resorts. John lived on-site until 1977, which

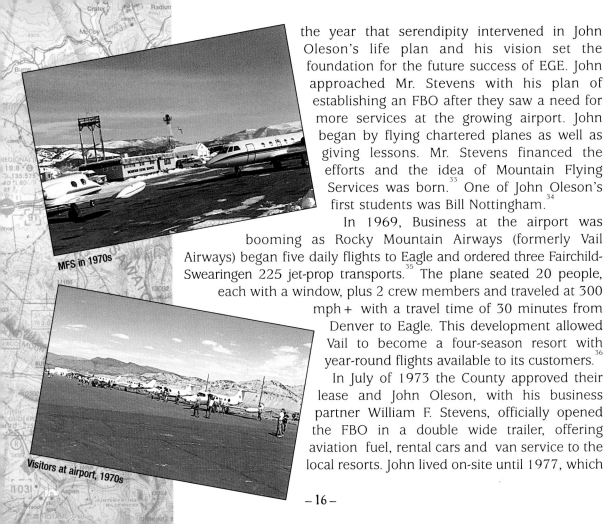

MFS in 1970s

Visitors at airport, 1970s

"I made more money pumping gas than flying it out [in lessons]."
– John Oleson

was convenient for the occasional middle-of-the-night call. In the winter, hours were generally 7 am – 5 pm, but in the summer MFS was open from 7 am – 9 pm.[37] Eventually, John realized that it was more profitable to service planes and guests than teach flight instruction as he comments, "I made more money pumping gas than flying it out [in lessons]". Even during the boycott and gas shortage in 1973, John pumped 3,000 gallons of fuel @ $0.48/gallon.[38] When asked about his most important achievement, John states that providing jet and fuel service to visitors flying into the airport was the most significant achievement during his tenure. Perhaps the most comical moment John recalls occurred at the expense of one of his employees. The incident transpired one summer day when a gal wearing a halter top was directing a plane into the terminal. As she was using hand maneuvers, her top fell down giving a free show and laugh to those who witnessed it. The pilot was caught off guard, watched her but not her signals, and taxied into the fuel area causing minor damage.[39]

Runway 8/26

Leonard Sinclair with Mike Lederhause's plane, 1980

Kathy, Edith, and Larry Lederhause, 1980

In 1977, Gypsum resident and entrepreneur Leonard Sinclair entered the picture with an enthusiasm for aviation. Not only did he satisfy his own aviation interests, Leonard established an FBO to meet the needs of visiting aircraft requiring mechanical assistance, 100-hour inspections, and also sold Piper airplanes. On the northwest side of the Eagle County Airport complex, Leonard poured a cement slab, erected a hangar, brought in a generator and an office trailer, and opened his business, without running water or electricity.[40]

Leonard remembers hauling prisoners to Aspen, with one armed officer accompanying them. At the time, the Eagle County jail only had eight beds so they had to farm out the prisoners. Leonard also remembers hauling corpses for the mortuary, and making trips to Pueblo transporting patients to the mental hospital.

Adding to his services, in 1978 Leonard Sinclair opened a flight school and used a Piper Cherokee Warrior for flight instruction. Leonard's mission was to teach students to fly safely. One of his first

"I believe gas was about 60 cents a gallon then and the airport was an enjoyable place to spend the day." – Mike Lederhause

students was Stewart Canada, a Vail realtor. Other students included Mike Lederhause, Sherry Brandon, Rex Schurenstedt (bought an Archer 180hp), Herby Schorp (bought a 181 Archer), and Richard Matthews (bought a Cherokee Warrior). Perhaps his youngest student, at the age of sixteen, was Vail resident Jamie Hoyt. Within one month Jamie was flying solo.[41] When Mike Lederhause bought his first plane, N3445Z, a 1960 Piper PA22/20 on February 1, 1980 for $5,000, he and Leonard had to make repairs to it before they could fly it home from its parking place on a private dirt landing strip in Strasburg, CO. It had rained and by the time the repairs were completed, the runway had become muddy and the aircraft became stuck. Mike had to get out of the aircraft and begin pushing it as Leonard applied the power. Once the plane started to move forward, Mike jumped in and they were soon airborne. After Leonard familiarized himself with the plane and its controls, he and Mike switched seats so Leonard could begin teaching Mike how to fly the plane. Mike recalls that "since there were no brakes on the right side, Leonard got a few gray hairs before I mastered the tail wheel." Mike describes flying with Leonard as "very enjoyable and educational since he had lots of experience flying. We had a few exciting times like the day the rubber bands in the landing gear broke and we ran off the runway. But mostly, it was enjoyable. I believe gas was about 60 cents a gallon then and the airport was an enjoyable place to spend the day." Since obtaining his pilot license, Mike has flown from the Atlantic Ocean to the Pacific Ocean, and from Mexico to the Arctic Circle.[42] Despite steady work and fulfilling a need at the airport, Leonard Sinclair closed his business in 1987 when the minimum standards were increased by the County Commissioners.

Air shows and open houses

The airport was a lot of fun, not just for travelers and local pilots, but for the community as well. In 1979, the Eagle County Airport sponsored an open house for the community. One of the perks was that local pilots Fred Collett and John Oleson gave rides to kids for a "penny a pound".[43] Pilots from all over brought their planes for display.[44]

In 1980, John Oleson completed a fundraising campaign and purchased an $80,000 instrument landing system through private donations. One benefactor was Oscar Wyatt, Chairman of Coastal States Gas in Houston, TX with a donation of $20,000. Tom Stone, chief pilot for HBE Corp., Totham Corporation of Houston, and Mike Wisenbaker of Midland, TX each donated $10,000 towards the system.[45] A few years later, John bought Mr. Stevens share of the business and became sole owner of MFS, another fortuitous moment in his life.[46]

The town of Vail and Mountain Flying Services were both growing very quickly between 1973 and 1986. The 5000' runway was considered very short and limited the amount of fuel planes could carry and it also limited the amount of fuel that could be sold. MFS and the County Commissioners (Dick Gustafson, Don Welch, and Jack Loughran) alike wanted to expand the airport quickly. All the players knew that if the runway was expanded, commercial jetliners would begin flying in to the airport. Their goal was to build a commercial terminal.

In 1985, the Eagle County Commissioners traveled to Washington, D.C. to present their request for funding for runway expansion. The airport at the time did not meet the minimum number of flight operations. Senator Bill Armstrong arranged for Commissioner Dick Gustafson to meet with General Temple at 5 PM on a Friday afternoon to discuss adding a National Guard Armory to the airport that would specialize in high-altitude training,

Big and little, 1984

which would boost the number of flight operations. This would make EGE eligible for FAA funding for expansion. Within about 45 minutes, Commissioner Gustafson in a phone call to Commissioner Don Welch, agreed on the terms and approval for the armory had been granted and funding for the runway was secured.[47] In April 1985, the site prep for airport expansion began and was completed by November 1985.[48] A year later, the paving and runway lighting was completed.[49]

In 1986, the County Commissioners increased the minimum standards required of businesses at the airport, which forced Leonard Sinclair to close his operations and John Oleson to invest several hundred thousand dollars in order to remain in business. To meet these requirements, John built a 22,500 square foot complex on the north side of the runway.[50]

On October 11, 1986, Eagle County Regional Airport's new runway 07/25 officially opened and the road off Cooley Mesa into the airport was named Eldon Wilson Road. The inaugural flight was piloted by Jerry Black in George Gillette's plane carrying County Commissioners Dick Gustafson, Bud Gates, and Don Welch. The commissioners were en route to promote the Eagle Valley area and airport at a tourism conference in New Orleans.[51]

Runway 7/25 Stats

Runway Specifications:
- 150' wide x 8000' long
- Dual wheel gross bearing capacity of 70,000 pounds

Improvements of the new runway included:
- Installation of a Precision Approach Path Indicator (PAPI) light system
- Runway End Identifier Lights (REILS)
- Lighted wind cone with segmented circle
- TVOR (Terminal VOR)
- Distance Measuring Equipment

Prior to expansion:	120 acres
After expansion:	521 acres

Land Acquisition:

Federal share	$1,452,393
Eagle County share	$ 840,127
Total cost of land	$2,292,520

Construction and Engineering Costs:

Federal share	$4,075,904
Eagle County share	$ 452,879

Total Project Costs:

Federal	$5,528,297
Eagle County	$1,293,006

Planes at MFS, circa 1977-1978

The expansion also included full parallel and connecting taxiway systems.

Source: *Eagle Valley Enterprise* Oct. 11, 1986

In October 1986, the FAA and state aviation authorities approved major commercial jet flights at EGE. This paved the way for direct flights from Los Angeles to EGE by Royal West Airlines. The inaugural flight on December 18, 1986 on a British Aerospace 146 carried 45 passengers to EGE. Just two days later, the Royal West Airlines flight was full with 85 passengers on board.[52]

Ribbon-cutting ceremony for the 1986 runway expansion

During these growing years, many well-known visitors arrived at the airport. In the original MFS facility, there was a wall-of-fame that showed snapshots of all the better-known guests and even those that thought they were well known. In one such instance, John Oleson recalls a time when one country western singer thought that upon arrival the Eagle County sheriff department—including all deputies—should escort him to Vail. The irony was that no one knew him here! John recalls that aside from this particular individual, most of the famous visitors were not demanding at all and were very personable. Another recollection John has is that many of the times, the famous people and celebrities were accompanied by companions that were not their spouses. During this time, these high-profile personalities were able to enjoy the solitude and paparazzi–free environment.

As the airport became busier a second Fixed Base Operator came onto the scene in 1987, joining Mountain Flying Services. Dr. Charles Howard built his business on the south side adjacent to the new runway.[54] As air traffic increased at the growing airport, there was a need for a radar system. In April of 1987 the Eagle County Commissioners traveled to Washington, D.C. to present their request for improved radar.[55] They met with National Guard, FAA, and DOT. This trip resulted in the radar facility on Red Table Mountain and eventually the new radar (that is scheduled for commission in June 2007). Flights to and from Eagle, Rifle, Aspen, and Avon all competed for the same airspace that was controlled by Denver Center. When these flights descended below 15,000 feet MSL (Mean Sea Level), the Minimum Reception Altitude (MRA) for the Denver radar, only one aircraft was allowed in the airspace at a time which created lengthy delays. The Red Table radar lowered the MRA to 10,300 feet MSL which reduced the delays and increased the number of aircraft per hour that could operate from these airports. The new radar at EGE will allow Denver Center to see the aircraft all the way to the runway, further increasing efficiency.[56]

In 1988, the jet center installed a new sprinkler system in the hangar. The Town of Gypsum required installation of a 1M gallon water tank on the hill. The Gypsum Fire Department required testing the new sprinkler system. The test was successful but it drained the tank and water went everywhere! The water washed down walls, roads, and created a vacuum in the city pipes leaving Gypsum without water for a time.[57] With progress, there are some pitfalls.

In July of 1988, Gillett Group purchased both Mountain Flying Services and Howard Air, including the rental car fleet maintained by Mountain Flying Services. Despite the growth of

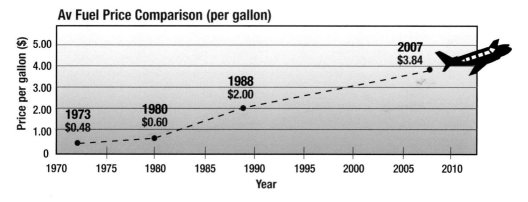

the airport, there was not enough business for both groups to survive.[58] Gillette and Howard became the two shareholders of the new Vail/Beaver Creek Jet Center. "I don't care where you go, you'll never find a better facility," promised Jerry Black, VP of Aviation for Gillette Group.[59] Black correctly predicted Vail's economic benefit but grossly underestimated the ability to make a profit for the jet center: "This is one more way to promote skiing in Vail. The Jet Center may not turn [a] profit but it will boost money spent in Vail and Beaver Creek."[60] Under the ownership of the Gillett Group, computerized state-of-the-art equipment was installed to provide weather and radar information, and a 40,000 square foot hangar was added.

Also during this time, United Airlines added daily air service from Denver during the summer months[61] and America West Airlines announced their intention of flying a Boeing 737 into the airport on a regular basis.[62]

Craig Colby, General Manager of the Vail/Beaver Creek Jet Center during the period from 1991-1998, remembers a time during one of the World Forums, the Prime Minister of

Mountain Flying Services during construction

Mountain Flying Services hangar with transportation fleet

Canada flew in to EGE along with dignitaries from Saudi Arabia and Washington, D.C. According to Craig, "Some guy had just landed and wanted to impress his girlfriend sitting in the car and started to drive across the runway to the FSS [before the tower was constructed]. The Saudi dignitaries arrived wearing their Armani suits with concealed firearms underneath. When the guy start[ed] honking his horn, the Saudi men in their Armani suits surround[ed] him with their firearms exposed. The guy quieted down real fast", laughs Craig. Another funny incident occurred during the Clinton administration. Craig recalls that "one of his people arrived in an Apache (or a Cobra) helicopter and took the aircraft for a cruise up the Eagle Valley. When they spotted a woman sunbathing at a Vail hotel, the aircraft began hovering. Immediately, the phone[s] began to ring with calls from citizens, managers of hotels, and Vail Associates employees wanting to know what was happening." Craig reports that he was hired to make the jet center profitable, but he also learned how to fly and had a cram course in aviation and airplanes. In explaining aviation, he describes it like this, "Aviation is rewarding but difficult, a dynamic industry, expensive, and has the most demanding customers in the world."[53]

Commercial air traffic was further enticed to EGE in 1989 when Vail Associates began financial guarantees to airlines with the Minimum Revenue Guarantee (MRG) program, spearheaded by Kent Myers.[63] The first year Vail Associates paid $35,000 to America West to meet the MRG, but every year after that the MRG was met or exceeded and no additional funds were paid to the airlines in the MRG program.[64] This achievement was due to the ability to connect travelers easily to Vail without the hassle of flying into Denver and traveling via car over two mountain passes during unpredictable winter weather. American Airlines began daily nonstop service between Eagle County Airport and American's major connecting hubs at Chicago and Dallas/Fort Worth during the 1990-91 ski season, serving the routes with twin-engine, 194-seat Boeing 757s, among the newest aircraft at the time in the carrier's fleet, according to American Airlines.[65]

The Influence of Gerald R. Ford

There is a direct correlation between the growing popularity of Eagle Valley and President Gerald Ford's influence. From the time that Mr. Ford first vacationed in Colorado in 1968, he began to draw attention to this area, not just on a national level, but worldwide. In 1982, Ford established the American Enterprise Institute (AEI) World Forum, a gathering of current and former world leaders and business executives to discuss political and business policies that impact current issues. Annually, this high-level gathering brings prominent guests from all over the world into Eagle Valley, flying through EGE.

President Ford's contribution to our airport was evident during the airport's growing years. Mr. Ford was very influential in obtaining the required approvals and equipment for the

Temporary tower installed for 1989 Alpine World Skiing Championships

airport and provided assistance to the County Commissioners. As Dick Gustafson reports, he had several taped interviews with Mr. Ford that were used in Washington, D.C. to support the expansion of the airport. During the time of the 1989 Alpine World Skiing Championships, of which Mr. Ford's influence weighed heavily in favor of Vail winning the host award, Mr. Ford in conjunction with FAA Director, Alan McCarter, also leveraged his influence in obtaining a temporary tower and radar for the airport.[66] The temporary tower was approved after Mr. Ford signed a letter penned by Dick Gustafson to then President Ronald Reagan. The temporary tower was in operation from mid-January to mid-February, 1989.

For twenty-five years, Mr. Ford chaired the Jerry Ford Invitational where top golfers and celebrities came to the valley to support local charities through the invitation-only golf tournament. In 1981, the Jerry Ford Celebrity Cup began bringing competitive skiers and celebrities together for a tournament in Vail.[67] Now called the Countrywide American Ski Classic, the event celebrates its 25th anniversary in 2007. Mr. Ford's love of skiing and his love of golf have made Eagle Valley a year-round attraction. The growth of this airport and this valley are linked to Gerald and Betty Ford and their efforts, and for that, we are grateful.

Photo courtesy Betty Ford Alpine Gardens

Mr. Ford entering *Tribute to Betty Ford*, Vail, Colorado, August 7, 2005

Mr. Ford and Dick Gustafson

In 1985, Eagle County set aside $300,000 toward acquiring a National Guard armory in a quick meeting in Washington, D.C. This meeting established the High-Altitude ARMG (Army National Guard) Aviation Training Site to conduct high-altitude and rough-terrain training.[68] Shortly thereafter, the State of Colorado gave Eagle County a grant in the amount of $300,000.[69]

The top reason for selecting this area is the altitude. Most combat situations occur in areas where altitude and heat, or both, degrade helicopter performance. These situations leave many pilots unprepared for their new flying assignments. HAATS provides foreign training for SATFA (Security Assistance Training Field Activity). Countries including Germany, Norway, Denmark, and Netherlands require this training.[70] A typical training week includes 7-1/2 flying hours for domestic training courses and 12-14 hours for foreign training classes. Students can bring their own aircraft such as CH-47 Chinook, UH-60 Blackhawk, AH-64 Apache helicopters, or they can use one of the four

UH-1 (Huey), five OH-58 (KIOWA), or the UH-60 (Blackhawk) aircraft that are maintained on site.[71]

HAATS trains aircrew members from National Guard, Active Army, US Navy, US Air Force, and NATO forces from Denmark, Germany, Netherlands, Norway, and Republic of Georgia with an emphasis on hazard mitigation, safety enhancement, and mission accomplishment.[72] Since the first class graduated in 1988, HAATS instructors have trained over 2000 students.[73] The training facility offers courses 40 weeks per year, working around the hunting season through an agreement with the Division of Wildlife. Currently, there are 18 full-time employees with plans to double that number in 2007. At the targeted staff level, there will be eleven instructor pilots, 20 mechanics, one flight operations manager, and the balance will be supply and life support personnel.[74]

In 2000, the Colorado National Guard paid for water and sewer services and Eagle County gave them another 14 acres and access to the landing strip. Recently, the County granted

HAATS a new 70-year lease. Part of the new lease agreement stipulates that within the first 15 years, they are required to build a new building containing the mess hall, administrative, classroom space, and hangar on the new land. Funding for this capital improvement was secured through Future Year Defense Planning. In 2011, they will begin a 3-phase construction/remodeling plan. Administrative, classroom space, and additional operation space will be created with additional accommodations for a larger hangar. Total space to be gained is 100,000 square feet for a cost of $35,090,000.[75]

HAATS training session

Sophisticated, Modern Airport

As improvements to the airport were made for the increased plane traffic, it had also reached a critical point to tap into the Town of Gypsum water and sewer system to accommodate the needs of the increased number of travelers through EGE. Finally, in 1992, city water and sewer services were extended to the airport.[76] It certainly is ironic that for so

many years, millionaires, dignitaries, famous entertainers, and wealthy clientele flew in to a full-service center but could not even drink the tap water and had limited bathroom facilities. This certainly was a critical improvement that was needed to catapult this airport into the sophisticated, modern airport that it is today.

Typical traffic before expansion, 1983

Post-expansion traffic, 1993

Commercial Enplanement Growth

	Annual Enplanements	% +/- Of Prior Year
1994	62,930	n/a
1995	85,503	35.87
1996	122,430	43.19
1997	174,533	42.56
1998	177,341	1.61
1999	173,241	-2.31
2000	188,745	8.95
2001	169,826	-10.02
2002	171,182	0.80
2003	170,601	-0.34
2004	193,382	13.35
2005	215,464	11.42
2006	218,105	1.23
	2,125,295	

Summer Enplanement Growth

Enplaned passengers by flight during the months of June thru September in the respective years.

	Total			Total
2000	8,272	2004	26,694
2001	6,071	2005*	36,846
2002	6,399	2006	30,673
2003	16,582		

* June 2005 enplanements up 31% over June 2004.

The addition of the summer flight program, designated "Fly Vail Summer", was implemented and backed by the local business community in 2003. The program began with a daily B-757 flight from Dallas/Fort Worth, operated by American Airlines. Since then, the "Fly Vail Summer" program has added large jet service from Chicago and Denver which has resulted in annual summer enplanement increases of more than 30,000 passengers annually in the months of June, July, August, and September. Enplanements during this period in 2002 totaled just over 6,000 and increased to more than 36,000 in 2005 during the same months.

Source: Chris Anderson, Airport Terminal Manager, Eagle County Regional Airport, January 26, 2007.

Another stride toward modernization occurred between December 1992 and January 1998 under the ownership of a group of 25 investors that purchased the FBO from Gillette. Some of the investors included Henry Kravis (of KKR), Mike Shannon and Larry Litchliter (both former Vail Associates officers), and Jeff Ross, who acted as FBO, inc.'s company president.[77] During their ownership, they built what is now Hangar IV and expanded the baggage terminal to accommodate another baggage carousel.

Eagle County Regional Airport Terminal

During his presidential campaign for the 1992 elections, Ross Perot flew into EGE. Knowing that Ross Perot likes to do his own thing, but wanting to get him in and out quickly without a lot of attention, Craig Colby watched for his arrival. Craig was sidetracked along the way and then realized that Mr. Perot had already landed. Craig searched the jet center and ventured down to the terminal and found him giving a stump speech to the crowd that had grown there.[78]

Baggage claim area, EGE terminal

Perhaps the most significant single improvement that contributed to the overall growth and sophistication at the airport occurred in November 1996 when Eagle County built the terminal with three gates financed by the airlines and bond issues for a total of $22,270,000, including the two gates that were added in 2001.[79] American Airlines contributed $7.5M.[80] The FAA approved Eagle County to fund its own terminal with a $3 per enplanement Passenger Facility Charge through 2006 totaling $4.5M. The other airlines also contributed to financing of the terminal through their rents.[81]

Since 1996, EGE has been financially self-sufficient. The revenue to operate is generated by users—passengers, airlines, tenants, and concessions.[82]

EGE Concessions

EAGLE SALOON

RED CANYON CAFE

Eagle Saloon, EGE

Red Canyon Cafe, EGE

EGE Gift Shop

Johnette's John

Despite the growth at the airport and the popularity of general aviation, the pilots were all disgruntled that restroom facilities for them were non-existent. Upset about lack of pilot restroom facilities, Ken Norman, who flew out of EGE from about 1969 to 2000, brought the problem to the public's and the County's attention. Mr. Norman wrote a letter to the editor complaining about the problem and the need to "go behind the hangar". Johnnette Phillips, County Commissioner from 1993 through 2000, made sure that improvements were made at the airport and garnered a deal between Eagle County and Vail Valley Jet Center. Construction of the new pilot lounge began in the fall of 1999 and was dedicated on December 18, 2000. Located on the north ramp, the facility includes not only a lounge with restrooms but a flight planning station as well. At the ribbon cutting ceremony, the Vail Valley Jet Center gave golden plungers to the commissioners and the facility was designated "Johnnette's John".

Ken Norman

Hugo Benson, Johnnette Phillips, Tom Stone and Mike Gallagher with golden plunger

Tom Stone, Johnnette Phillips, and Jim Elwood

Modernization plans continued with the addition of the EGE Tower, which was commissioned in November 2003. Costing $2.2M and taking one year to build, the tower controls the airspace 2,500 feet up with a five-mile radius.[83] The tower is 102' to the top of the roof and 90' to the cab floor. The control cab is taller than a standard tower for this size of an airport. There are four year-round employees that staff the tower from 7 am – 7 pm, except during the winter holidays when it is staffed from 7 am – 11 pm, with the help of an additional seasonal employee to assist with the increased winter traffic.[84]

Efforts began in 2004 to add an electronic instrument landing system (ILS). The ILS was installed in 2006 and serves as a precision navigational approach aid. With the use of electronics on the ground and displays in the cockpit the pilots are able to intercept a narrow approach path which guides their aircraft directly to the runway touchdown area. Even with low visibility the pilot is able

Eagle Tower

to safely navigate their aircraft through the surrounding terrain by using the ILS, increasing the reliability of flights in and out of EGE. Other benefits include a shorter approach time into the airport by five minutes per plane which enables more planes to land.[85]

2006 Runway Expansion

Another major contributing factor to growth at the Eagle County Regional Airport occurred in April 2004 when a decision to extend the runway 1000' (from 8000' to 9000') was granted which allows heavier planes to land and take off, and provides an even greater safety margin for departing aircraft, especially in warmer summer temperatures.[86] The extension is expected to be completed in 2008.

In July 2006, the BI-6 radar was installed, which picks up signals from incoming planes under 10,500 feet. This feature allows Denver Center to guide aircraft all the way to the runway.[87] (More information on the radar can be found on page 26 and 56).

Passengers in the baggage claim area of EGE

VAIL VALLEY JET CENTER

N800JH

December 2005 Employee Photo

In the spring of 1988, George Gillette purchased both FBOs on the field. The terminal on the south side became the Vail/Beaver Creek Jet Center and the Mountain Flying Service facility on the north side was leased to Colorado National Guard. Jerry Black, General Manager and Vice President of Aviation (Chief Pilot), announced that the Jet Center "aim[s] to offer first–rate service to its customers," which it did for ten years.

On January 20, 1998, the Vail Beaver Creek Jet Center was purchased by an investor group consisting of Jim Allen, E.B. Chester, Bill Esrey, Fred Hamilton, Lisa Ireland, and George Wiegers. A new company was formed and the FBO was renamed the Vail Valley Jet Center.

Today, the VVJC serves Eagle County as one of the premier FBOs in the country. The Jet Center provides a wide range of aviation services including luxury terminal, conference room and business center space; fuel, hangar, deicing and ramp services; and first class on-site catering provided by JetStream Seasonings. The Jet Center also provides a wide range of aircraft maintenance services. Duncan Avionics and VVJC's mechanics are highly qualified and trained to work on everything from Cessna 172s to Boeing 757 aircraft. Since 2002, the VVJC has been consistently voted one of the top FBOs in the nation in *Aviation International News* and *Professional Pilot Magazine.*[89] Paul Gordon, President and General Manager, attributes this success to the dedicated group of employees that work tirelessly to make the FBO and the airport one of the best in the nation.

April 2006 – *Aviation International News* ranks Vail Valley Jet Center #19 in "The Top 40 American FBO Survey".

Reprinted with permission of Aviation International News © 2006

The Company's Chairman and CEO, Jim Allen, has been flying out of EGE since 1965 and was one of the founding members of the ECAA. From the beginning, Jim had many visions for the airport. Since 1998, the VVJC has partnered with Eagle County in building a Customer Lounge and Flight Planning Facility, as well as a Self-Fueling Facility on the north side of the airfield. The VVJC has also worked closely with Eagle County to bring US Customs to the airfield and built more ramp and hangar space to meet the growing needs of the Airport. Jim Allen once said, "One day, Eagle County will become an international airport." Slowly, that vision is becoming a reality as well.

VAIL VALLEY
JET CENTER

After the terrorist attacks on September 11, 2001, passenger requirements and security restrictions tightened. This restriction on commercial air travel made general aviation a more attractive option. As a result, business at FBOs across the country increased. The inconvenience of new restrictions on airline travel drove people and companies to invest in general aviation.

These restrictions, combined with technological advances in composite manufacturing, engine technology and improved avionics has led to the development of an entirely new generation of business jets.

Very light jets (VLJs) will also create additional business growth and bring more travelers through the airport in years to come. According to Ken Hespe, a spokesman for the National Consortium for Aviation Mobility, by 2010, 8,300 VLJs will be in service for

Dr. Jack Eck, left, with Jim Allen, Chairman/CEO of VVJC – Dr. Eck has been flying his Stinson out of EGE since the 1970s.

Dr. Jack Eck

passengers wishing to avoid the hassles of commercial flights.[90] Paul Gordon explains, "VLJs have extremely fuel efficient, quiet engines, hold 4-6 passengers, and will continue to boost general aviation".[91] The Federal Aviation Administration has predicted that the use of private business jets will triple because of VLJs' lower costs.[92]

Celebrating the opening of the self-fueling station, December 13, 2005

EGE Today

In a continued effort to provide the ultimate in customer service and convenience, Eagle County Airport is served by six major airlines year-round with nonstop destinations to 14 major U.S. cities, and offers free wireless internet service throughout the terminal.

Winter:	American	Northwest	Continental	Delta	United	USAirways
Summer/Fall:	American	United				
Spring:	United					

AmericanAirlines®

 nwa NORTHWEST AIRLINES®

Continental Airlines

UNITED

▲**Delta**

 **U·S AIRWAYS**

US Customs and Border Protection provides customs services at VVJC for private aircraft. Through a partnership with VVJC and Eagle County, a customs agent is assigned to EGE and meets the passengers and crew planeside, clearing international flights arriving at Eagle County Airport.

At the time of publication, there are 15 year-round Eagle County employees at the airport.[93] This figure does not include airline employees. In high season, there are more than 500 security badges issued, 300 of them are terminal badges. The Vail Valley Jet Center currently has 54 employees.[94]

Deicing before departure

Photos courtesy Brent Bingham

A winter scene at EGE

Behind-the-Scene Key Equipment and Personnel

Harry Hurd

Looking Ahead

EGE is currently undergoing construction efforts to keep up with the growth of this booming airport. There are two separate expansion projects in the works. The biggest project includes the runway expansion, encompassed with three phases.[95] The second expansion project is a three-phase terminal expansion project.

Terminal Expansion

During peak season, the airport terminal is filled to capacity. Officials at EGE are currently working on a three-phase terminal expansion plan to accommodate the need of the visitors as well as making improvements to the baggage area.[96] Work is underway to design and construct a structure that will enclose and heat the baggage sorting area, presently outside of the terminal. Inside the terminal, additional food and beverage service will be added including kiosks and a coffee shop, news and gift shops, and more than 200 additional seats for waiting passengers. These improvements are scheduled for 2007. Phase II of the terminal expansion calls for widening of the TSA checkpoint area and increasing the square footage of the food and beverage area through a rearrangement of existing space. The final phase includes an evaluation to determine if there is a need to physically expand the terminal and what design would best suit the expansion. Expansion options include building a second level on the terminal, pushing out the terminal walls to the north, and extending the terminal to the west to accommodate additional gates. This phase is expected to be addressed in 2008.

Phase I
Summer 2006

The initial phase included what has become known as one of the largest earth moving projects in the state's history, moving 1.75M yards of dirt. Dirt was hauled to lengthen the primary runway (Runway 7/25) from across Cooley Mesa Road from Saddle Ridge. This was a mutually beneficial arrangement since Saddle Ridge Development needed it removed for their resort and golf community.

Phase II
Summer 2007

The next phase includes moving the final 0.75M yards of the needed dirt from the same location and prep the area for paving.

Phase III
Summer 2008

The final phase includes paving, striping, lighting, and opening of the lengthened runway.

Total cost: $25M
Funded by:
  95% FAA
  5% split between Eagle County and CDOT through CDOA (Colorado Division of Aviation: the aeronautics group that promotes safe and profitable airports in Colorado)

The runway length will grow from 8000' to 9000' and provide the following benefits:

- Give pilots a full 9000' for takeoff.
- Provide increased level of safety overall.
- The standard departure procedure calls for a left-hand turn over Cottonwood Pass. The lengthened runway will increase the takeoff distance available (TODA), affording aircraft a greater initial climb rate, which will position the aircraft higher and further from surrounding terrain.
- Additional TODA will allow greater takeoff capacity, which will increase year-round passenger capacities

New Radar

Due to the frequency of inclement weather and the number of diverted planes, officials began plans in 1985 to add a radar system, which is scheduled for commissioning in June 2007. During inclement weather, the number of landings is reduced from 16 per hour to just six.[97] According to a 2000/2001 study, landing diversions total $63M so it was economically crucial to obtain the new radar.[98] The new radar will reduce the number of planes diverted and thereby keep the revenue generating through the airport, the airport businesses, and the Eagle Valley. Taking more than six years to finance, Eagle County's $1.5M share of the $6M radar system was met in November 2004, at which time the FAA took over the logistics of obtaining and installing the system.[99]

Currently, Denver Air Traffic Control Center (ARTCC), commonly referred to as "Denver Center", hands off aircraft to the local EGE tower, which then provides local separation of aircraft on approach and departure.[100]

New radar system scheduled for commissioning in June 2007

Famous Faces

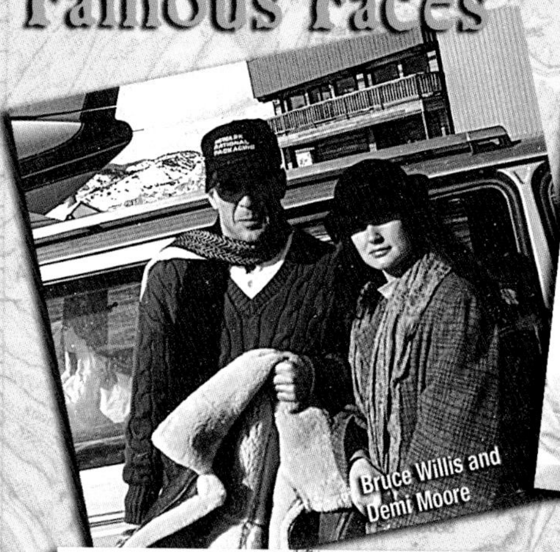

Bruce Willis and Demi Moore

Clint Eastwood

Alan Greenspan

Arnold Palmer

Jackie Gleason

Dinah Shore and Wayne Rogers

Glenn Campbell

Henry Kissinger

Cast of
Ultimate Thrill

Hal Linden

Gregory Peck

Gary Hart

Flip Wilson

Jerry Pate

John Denver

Robert Redford

Michael Landon

A.G. SPANOS CONSTRUCTION INC.

Bob and Dolores Hope

Tip O'Neil

Jamie Farr

Gerald and Betty Ford

John Glenn

Sammy Davis Jr.

John Conally

George C. Scott

Telly Savalas

Oprah Winfrey

Trivia

- VVJC sells 100LL (100 Low Lead Piston Aircraft Fuel) at one of the cheapest prices in the nation at their self-service station.

- VVJC on service: Call ahead, we'll get the plane out for you, check the fuel level, fill it, and even get the catering on board for you. You just show up and then you're on your way.

- 40% of commercial passenger share in a calendar year is with American Airlines due to their deep flight schedule in the winter.

- 50 cents from every gallon of fuel goes to EGE for takeoff and landing costs.

- Did you know that the planes at night can control the landing strip lights by clicking the microphone?

- How many steps are there from the entrance to the tower up to the cab floor? (a)

- How many hours does John Oleson have flying? (b)

- In 1987, EGE had 23,238 visitors. These visitors spent more than $4M on food, lodging, ground transportation, and entertainment.

- In the early 1990s, EGE closed runway 8/26.

(a) There are 171 steps. (b) John has more than 4,000 hours flying single and multi-engine planes.

• On September 11, 1997 EGE celebrated its 50-year anniversary. While never a pilot but always an aviation aficionado, Eldon Wilson received accolades for his vision and persistence. This EGE pioneer focused his energies on creating an airport in the area and persistently lobbied commissioners to fund it. "Eldon Wilson was the visionary who pushed the airport along", recalled long-time Eagle resident and retired businessman Harold Koonce.[101]

• The Colorado Department of Transportation estimated that the Eagle County Regional Airport contributed $440M to the local and state economics through tourism dollars and wages in 2003.[102]

• In 2003, EGE had 171,000 commercial passengers and 70,000 charter/private passengers.[103]

• In 2005, EGE commercial enplanements increased 11% over 2004, totaling 215,464.[104] This is the first year that EGE surpassed the 200,000 mark.

• Al Oleson's great-grandson, Jeffrey Williams, and Eldon Wilson's great-grandson, Jeff Ruggeberg, are both Captains with Frontier Airlines. Both pilots attended Eagle Valley High School.[105]

References

[1] Eagle County Courthouse, Record of Sale.

[2] *Eagle Valley Enterprise*, August 14, 1931.

[3] *Eagle Valley Enterprise*, May 5, 1939.

[4] Charlynn Williams, email to the author, 25 January 2007.

[5] Sale Contract, V. Julius Oleson, 1921.

[6] Sale Contract, V. Julius Oleson, 1921.

[7] *Eagle Valley Enterprise*, 1921 article.

[8] *Eagle Valley Enterprise*, 1921 article.

[9] Charlynn Williams, Personal interview, 24 January 2007.

[10] "Landing Field to be Inspected Next Sunday" *Eagle Valley Enterprise*, August 4, 1939.

[11] State Air Squadron to Visit Local Airport Soon" *Eagle Valley Enterprise*, June 1939.

[12] "Landing Field to be Inspected Next Sunday" *Eagle Valley Enterprise*, August 4, 1939.

[13] Allan Nottingham, Personal interview 20 June 2006.

[14] *Eagle Valley Enterprise*, June 1939.

[15] "Memorial to Honor World War II Lend-Lease Program Unveiled", *Alaska* magazine, February 2007, vol. 73, no. 1: page 15.

[16] *Alaska* magazine.

[17] *Eagle Valley Enterprise*, 1951.

[18] "Gov. Knous Will Attend Dedication" *Eagle Valley Enterprise*, Sept. 12, 1947.

[19] Eagle County Courthouse, Title Deed.

[20] FAA Northwest Mountain Region, Administrator's Fact Book.

[21] Allan Nottingham, Personal interview 20 June 2006.

[22] "Gov. Knous Will Attend Dedication" *Eagle Valley Enterprise*, Sept. 12, 1947.

[23] "Eagle County May Maintain Airport" *Eagle Valley Enterprise*, April 6, 1961.

[24] "Eagle County May Maintain Airport" *Eagle Valley Enterprise*, April 6, 1961.

[25] "Eagle County May Maintain Airport" *Eagle Valley Enterprise*, April 6, 1961.

[26] *Eagle Valley Enterprise*, Jan. 1, 1962.

[27] "Eagle County May Maintain Airport" *Eagle Valley Enterprise*, April 6, 1961.

[28] *Eagle Valley Enterprise*, Feb. 16, 1966.

[29] *Eagle Valley Enterprise*, June [undated], 1966.

[30] *Eagle Valley Enterprise*, undated article.

[31] *Vail Trail*, Aug. 11, 1967.

[32] John Oleson Personal interview 20 June 2006.

[33] Oleson.

[34] Oleson.

[35] "Ski Country Airline Goes for New Jets" *Eagle Valley Enterprise*, Feb. 10, 1969.

[36] "Ski Country Airline Goes for New Jets" *Eagle Valley Enterprise*, Feb. 10, 1969.

[37] Oleson.

[38] Oleson.

[39] Oleson.

[40] Leonard Sinclair Personal interview 4 September 2006.

[41] Sinclair.

[42] Mike Lederhause, email to author, 14 October 2006.

[43] Sinclair.

[44] Sinclair.

[45] Oleson.

[46] Oleson.

[47] Dick Gustafson, email to the author, 18 January 2007.

[48] Chris Anderson, email to the author, 24 October, 2006.

[49] *Eagle Valley Enterprise*, May 8, 1986.

[50] *Vail Trail*, Jan. 2, 1987.

[51] Gustafson.

[52] *Vail Daily*, Sept. 17, 1987.

[53] *Eagle Valley Enterprise*, April 16, 1987.

[54] Oleson.

[55] *Eagle Valley Enterprise*, April 16, 1987.

[56] Lee Weatherbee, ATC Manager, Eagle County Regional Airport, Personal interview 17 August 2006.

[57] Craig Colby Personal interview 9 September 2006.

[58] Oleson.

[59] Jerry Black as quoted in *Eagle Valley Enterprise*, Aug. 4, 1988.

[60] Black.

[61] *Avon/Beaver Creek Times*, Aug. 2, 1989.

[62] *Eagle Valley Enterprise*, Aug. 3, 1989.

[63] *Eagle Valley Enterprise*, Oct. 16, 1986.

[64] Kent Myers Personal interview 17 August 2006.

[65] Al Becker, Corporate Communications, American Airlines, Press release dated May 2, 1990.

[66] Dick Gustafson, email to the author, 18 January 2007.

[67] John Dakin, Vail Valley Foundation, email to the author, 24 January 2007.

[68] Gustafson.

[69] Gustafson.

[70] Major Joshua Day, HAATS Commander, Colorado Army Guard Bureau, Personal interview, 6 June 2006.

[71] Day.

[72] Day.

[73] Day.

[74] Day.

[75] Day.

[76] Oleson.

[77] Myers.

[78] Craig Colby Personal interview 9 September 2006.

[79] Chris Anderson, Airport Administration Manager, Eagle County Regional Airport, email to the author, 17 August 2006.

[80] Paul Gordon, President and General Manger, Vail Valley Jet Center, email to the author, 25 July 2006.

[81] Gordon.

[82] Chris Anderson, Airport Administration Manager, Eagle County Regional Airport, personal interview, 8 August 2006.

[83] Anderson and Lee Weatherbee, ATC Manager, Midwest ATC, Personal interview 17 August 2006.

[84] Weatherbee.

[85] *Vail Daily*, Jan. 27, 2004.

[86] Chris Anderson, email to the author, 24 January 2007.

[87] Weatherbee.

[88] Colby.

[89] Gordon.

[90] *Washington Post*, 1994, ttp://www.washingtonpost.com/wp-dyn/articles/A15663-2004Nov26.html.

[91] Gordon.

[92] Cnet News.com, http://news.com.com/Cheap + microjets + take + to + the + skies/2100-11395_3-6065935.html.

[93] Anderson.

[94] Gordon.

[95] Chris Anderson, email to the author, 26 October 2006.

[96] Chris Anderson, email to the author 12 January 2007.

[97] *Vail Daily*, Jan. 27, 2004.

[98] *Vail Daily*, Nov. 14, 2004.

[99] Anderson, personal interview, 8 August 2006.

[100] Anderson.

[101] *Eagle Valley Enterprise*, Vol. 101, No. 52.

[102] Colorado Department of Transportation.

[103] Eagle County website, May 31, 2006.

[104] Anderson.

[105] Williams.